IMAGES
of England

KIDDERMINSTER

Baxter House, High Street, when it was under the ownership of Joseph Ray.

IMAGES
of England

KIDDERMINSTER

Compiled by
Robert Barber

TEMPUS

First published 1999
Reprinted 1999
Second Reprint 1999
Copyright © Robert Barber, 1999

Tempus Publishing Limited
The Mill, Brimscombe Port,
Stroud, Gloucestershire, GL5 2QG

ISBN 0 7524 1683 9

Typesetting and origination by
Tempus Publishing Limited
Printed in Great Britain by
Midway Clark Printing, Wiltshire

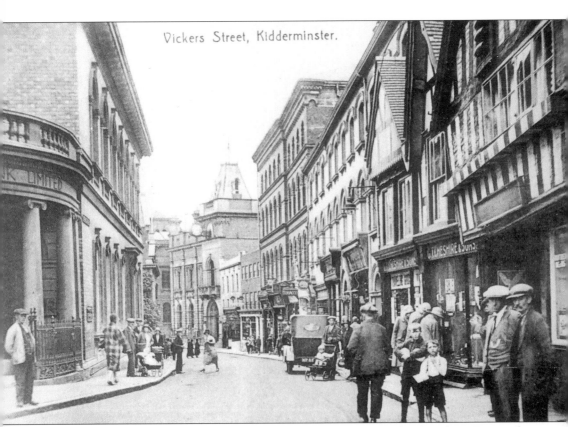

Vicar Street in the 1920s. The public house in the right foreground is the Three Tuns and next door is the printers, Cheshire & Sons. Note the misspelling of the street name on the postcard.

Contents

Coal being unloaded from a canal barge near St Mary's church, probably for Carpet Trades boiler house.

J.R. Timmis

Foreword

After being born, brought up and having spent all my working life in Kidderminster, I was very pleased to be asked to write the foreword for this book.

Before the two World Wars, many of Kidderminster's shopkeepers were born and bred locally. They were aware of and dedicated to their customers needs. Shops were open from early morning to late evening for six days a week.

The town has changed greatly since the Second World War with many buildings razed to the ground. Today's younger generation may not remember many of the views shown in the book, while many of the more modern buildings have yet to become history.

Despite a growth in the number of supermarkets, the town centre still has independent retail shops and we rely on those remaining to give special interest locally. There is a certain appeal when one realises they have just walked into such a shop and these still attract the discerning shopper.

As we will soon be entering the twenty-first century, the author asked me to comment on how I see the town's future – I believe it has a great future. Stronger competition than ever requires special marketing skills at Wyre Forest Council to encourage shoppers into Kidderminster, Bewdley and Stourport-on-Severn, and to attract shoppers from outlying areas. 'People Movers' (modern, easily accessible buses) transport motorists from free parking areas to the newly enlarged town centre. This will match out-of-town trading, with traffic wardens to welcome shoppers into town!

Enjoy reading this wonderfully illustrated and well-written book. How fortunate we are in having Mr Robert Barber's interest and recollections in recording so much of the history of Kidderminster's shops and businesses.

John Robert Timmis
W.E. Timmis Hardware & Ironmongery (1865-31 December 1986)
Coventry Street, Kidderminster

Introduction

The main purpose of this book is to inform the reader of some fine shops and businesses that have traded in Kidderminster over the past 150 years. The majority of these have ceased to be, though a few have survived. Information about the business owners themselves, including where they came from and where they learnt their trade, can be found in many instances. There are also photographs of the premises (mainly outside views, but in some cases the inside), as well as the employers and the employees.

When I approached some of the local businesses for information about themselves it amazed me how readily they produced old photographs (from a back room in some cases) and entrusted them to a total stranger for the purpose of having them copied. It was quite unbelievable and went a long way towards making the task of compiling this book easier.

One of the most exciting finds while researching this book was a Castle-Three motor car which was made in Kidderminster, just after the First World War. It is in excellent condition and it is possible that only one other Castle-Three survives. Beaulieu Motor Museum sold one in the 1960s but its whereabouts are unknown. Heartfelt thanks are due to Mrs D. Knight, the owner of the vehicle, for allowing it to be brought to Kidderminster to be shown at Hartlebury Museum from May to August 1999.

In conclusion, interesting shops make an interesting town. In these days of supermarkets and superstores the little specialist trader is becoming a rare commodity. Hopefully this book will rekindle memories of the days when a 'super-market' was a collection of trestle tables where a lot of bargains could be had.

Robert Barber

One

New Road to Oxford Street

Worcester Road island, *c.* 1956. This beautifully manicured island greeted travellers who approached the town from Worcester.

Castle Motor Co. Ltd. The works as they appeared during the 1920s in New Road with the main entrance in Dixon Street.

The Castle Motor Company was established in 1907 by Stanley and Laughton Goodwin and by the 1920s had the reputation of being the finest equipped garage in the Midlands. Any make of motor car or motorcycle could be repaired and any kind of motor body could be built for either commercial or personal vehicles. Motorists' accessories could be supplied from stock or within a few days of receipt of order. The company was also the official repairer for the AA and the RAC and could supply any make of motorcycle or car from the 'Humble Henry' to models that were dignified, high-powered, expensive, silent and elegant.

In 1919 the company's founders decided to produce a motor vehicle of their own in an effort to capture some of the fast growing market for personal transport. The vehicle which they produced was a handsome three-wheeler with an open top and a water-cooled four-cylinder engine made by Dorman of Stafford. To complement the model name, the radiator incorporated a castle tower in its outline. As the vehicle was really a 'cycle-car', it was exhibited at the 1919 Olympia motorcycle show where it made a huge impact and in excess of 3,000 orders were received.

Realistically, however, it was beyond the capability of the Castle Motor Company to meet such a demand. The suppliers of the engine could only supply a few units, so they looked elsewhere and chose a Belgian-made Peters engine which was used until the end of production. To add to the problems, the Ford Motor Company issued a writ for an infringement of their patented drive mechanism and, as a result, this had to be redesigned. While these events were taking place, the majority of the people who had made an order were beginning to lose interest. In an effort to prevent this the company entered the vehicle into a number of sporting events, particularly hill climbs, and had a certain amount of success. The prototype car was entered in The Motorcycling Club's annual London to Edinburgh run. In advance of this event the makers set the vehicle additional tasks such as a climb of Buttertubs Pass in North Yorkshire – still a formidable climb today. The little Castle romped up and showed itself to be a very worthy competitor. All these efforts proved to be in vain, however, as the final blow came when the

Austin Seven went into production in 1922. From that moment on, the Castle-Three, along with a host of other small manufacturers, was doomed. In all about 350 Castle-Three's were produced and it is thought that only two survive. There is a four-wheeled version in the Birmingham Science Museum.

If the Castle Motor Company had not gone into car production, there is a distinct possibility that they would still be in business today in a similar vein to Carmichael's of Worcester, producing bodies for vehicles such as fire engines and ambulances. It is ironic that they produced such a worthy product and received far more orders than they imagined possible, only to fail. Surely it was better to receive too many orders than not enough!

In comparison to Castle's situation, the Morgan Motor Company have survived for years by producing just a few units per annum. Indeed, that seems to be part of the magic: you can have one if you are prepared to wait.

By 1924 Stanley and Laughton Goodwin had set up their own garage businesses. Laughton was the sole Midland distributor of Hudson Super Six and Essex cars at his premises in George Street and Stanley had acquired Ford and Singer agencies, trading at premises in New Road. In 1928 Laughton had become the joint Midland distributor for Chrysler cars while Stanley was still a Ford agent in New Road. It is worth noting that the Castle Motor Company was still in business in New Road and had a motorcycle showroom and sports outfitting shop at 19 Vicar Street and showrooms at 63 Broad Street, Birmingham, and 18 The Tything, Worcester.

Four years later the Castle Motor Company was no longer in business but Bert Matthews, a former employee, had opened a filling station and garage at Foley Park. The petrol station is still in business and does much to help maintain low petrol prices in the area. Bill Lewis, who had been the works manager, joined Stanley Goodwin for a time before opening a garage business in New Road with Jack Baggott, another former employee of the Castle Motor Company. They are probably best remembered as BSA Motorcycle and Standard Triumph agents. The latter was secured around the time that the Triumph Herald, a unique car that perhaps does not look out of date nearly forty years later, first appeared on the market. Finally, there was Fred Fry who opened a garage in Tenbury Wells.

The showroom in New Road. Note the tramlines in the foreground.

The workshop where general repairs were carried out. Standing at the machine in the left foreground is Fred Fry, in the centre wearing the cap is Jack Baggott, kneeling on the right is Bert Matthews and on the extreme right is Bill Lewis.

Malvern Hill climb, c. 1920. To keep the potential customers interest alive while the Castle Motor Company was trying to meet the 3,000 orders, the Castle-Three was entered into various competitive events. The two competitors here are Bill Lewis and probably C.P. Joseland.

A Castle-Three in Mill Street in 1922. This is the start of the Junior Car Club's Manchester run.

This Prince Henry Vauxhall belonged to Sir Herbert Smith of Witley Court and appears to be undergoing major restoration.

Left: The former site of the Castle Motor Company in 1999, still looking very much the same as it appeared in the 1920s. Laughton Goodwin (below left) was the company's General Manager. Stanley Goodwin (below right) was the General Manager and the designer of the Castle-Three Runabout.

A line of Castle-Threes wait for their bodywork.

The general repair shop.

CASTLE-THREE RUNABOUT.

SPECIFICATION.

ENGINE.—Four Cylinders, cast *en block* 62 m/m bore and 100 m/m stroke, giving 1.207 c.c. The valves which are *side by side*, are inclined at the side of the Cylinders in order to obtain as small a pocket as possible over the valve heads. The tappets are adjustable, and are operated by a silent chain (adjustable) driven camshaft.

IGNITION.—High Tension Variable.

CONTROL. — Foot accelerator, inter-connected with control on dash.

CARBURETTOR.—Solex, horizontal type.

COOLING.—Cooling is by Thermo-Syphon through liberal water jackets and handsome radiator of approved design.

LUBRICATION.—Lubrication to the Engine is Automatic by means of a geared type of pump which delivers oil under pressure to the main bearings, also maintaining correct oil level in the troughs from which the big end bearings are lubricated through scoops at their extremities. Owing to the connecting rods being tubular, the gudgeon pins and pistons are lubricated by the oil travelling through them. Lubrication to all other working parts of the chassis, other than the rear axle case and gear box, is reduced to practically nothing by means of patent oil-less bearings which need no lubrication whatever.

BACK AXLE and FINAL DRIVE (Patented).

Specially designed bevel drive, totally enclosed, running in oil, and provided with extra large ball bearings throughout. Bevel and Crown Wheels are adjustable for wear, etc., and easily detachable.

Rear Wheel is detachable in a few moments by the use of a single spanner and is interchangeable with front wheels (a most important point).

By this method we claim to have once and for all eliminated the hitherto great objection to three-wheeled vehicles.

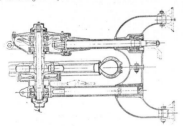

CHANGE SPEED GEAR.—(Patent applied for)—By Epicyclic System, giving two forward speeds (direct on top) and reverse. The complete revolving unit is carried by two large ball bearings and is adjustable for end thrust. Adjustment or withdrawal of the bands or complete withdrawal of internal unit being extremely easy.

This type of gear has been chosen for three reasons :—
  (1) Noviceproofness and ease of manipulation.
  (2) Extreme low cost of upkeep.
  (3) Efficiency.
Pedals adjustable for length.

CASTLE-THREE RUNABOUT

FRONT AXLE.—Tubular Section with " inclined " type of steering heads, with ball thrust bearings to swivel heads.

CHASSIS.—Pressed Steel side members, channel section.

SPRINGS.—Front : Quarter Elliptic.
Rear : Semi-Elliptic, flat type and under-slung, 42in. long.

WHEELS.—Goodyear all steel, interchangeable all round.

TYRES.—26 x 3 Cord, Rear and Spare Wheel, 26 x 3 Canvas. Front.

BRAKES.—Foot brake operating on drum running in oil in gear box—and hand brake operating internal expanding shoes on rear wheel—both easily adjustable for wear, and highly efficient.

STEERING.—By planetary gear reduction and adjustable for rake, giving perfect and extremely light control under all conditions.

BODY—Standard.—Roomy two-seater with flush tapering sides, and provision for large amount of luggage, etc.

EQUIPMENT.—Hood, screen, dynamo lighting set, horn, tool-kit, jack, pump and number plates.

WHEEL BASE.—8ft. 6in. Track, 4ft. 1in.

PRICE

Complete with Dynamo Lighting Set,
Spare Wheel and Tyres.

£225.

Dickey Seat, £5 extra.   Discs, £6 6s. 0d. extra.

An advertisement that gives a wide range of information and specifications for the Castle-Three Runabout.

THE CASTLE MOTOR CO. LTD.

CHAIRMAN:
SIR HERBERT SMITH, BART.
MANAGING DIRECTOR:
LAUGHTON C. GOODWIN.
SECRETARY:
WILLIAM GILMOUR.

Works and Registered
Offices: NEW ROAD,
Showrooms:
VICAR ST. KIDDERMINSTER.
TELEGRAMS:
"CASTLE MOTOR, KIDDERMINSTER."
TELEPHONE Nos 226, 227 & 168

Automobile and General Engineers

Our Ref. LD/MA.

Your Ref.

68. BROAD STREET.
BIRMINGHAM.

MANAGER; BIRMINGHAM OFFICE: HAROLD GOODWIN.

TELEGRAMS: "CASMOCOL"
TELEPHONE: -784 MID.
Mid.3150.
Septr. 25th/24.

Donald Rowe Esq,
The Briars,
Thorold Road,
Bitherne Park,
Southampton.

Dear Sir:—

   With reference to the postscript to your letter addressed
to our Kidderminster Depot attached hereto, we can offer you
a Castle Three, just overhauled and repainted, in excellent order
for £50.0.0. Also a Castle Three converted into a four
wheeler by the addition of a Wrigley back axle and three speed
reverse gear box, for £60.0.0.

   Both these cars are in excellent order and have been used
solely by our own salesmen.

   Trusting to hear from you and assuring you always of our
best attention.,

          Yours faithfully,

          p.p. THE CASTLE MOTOR COMPANY LTD.,

                              MANAGER.

A letter dated 25 September 1924. Donald Rowe of Southampton had purchased a new Castle-Three, with the registration CR 5868, for a price of well over £200 and was offered another one for just 50. Quite a devaluation!

This was the Castle-Three that belonged to Donald Rowe of Southampton. It was discovered bricked up in a derelict church by a building developer in the 1960s. It was purchased and lovingly restored by Mr C. Knight around 1969. Its nickname is 'Donald'.

Seated in the car is Mrs D. Knight who gave permission for the car to be loaned to the Hartlebury Museum.

The staff of the Castle Motor Works, *c.* 1920.

Lewis & Baggott's garage, New Road, *c.* 1956. The management and staff are, from left to right: E. Bennett, G. Turner, J. Mullard, C. Watts, R. Galloway, Bill Lewis, Mrs Humphries, R. Lewis, Jack Baggott and Mr Oakes, who owned a café nearby. The special occasion was the redecoration of the premises in BSA livery.

Thomas & Wilks were pump makers and well sinkers with premises in New Road. They were known in Kidderminster and throughout the country as artesian well borers of eminence, experts in the piercing of strata and the makers of quality geological surveys. The business was originally founded in the 1800s by a Mr Jinston. Later in the same century he was succeeded by Mr Thomas who was joined around 1880 by Mr Wilks. Mr Wilks became the sole proprietor during the early 1900s. The majority of artesian wells in Kidderminster would have been bored by Thomas & Wilks. The deepest well they sunk in the early 1900s was 300 feet but they had the capability to go deeper if required.

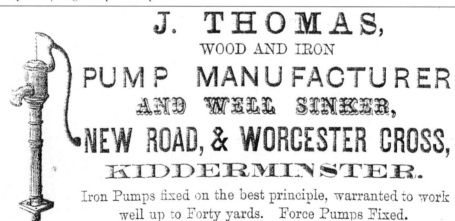

An advertisement from before Mr Wilks joined the firm.

Thomas & Wilks drill for a soft water source at Hoo Brook to provide steam for the engines of the Great Western Railway.

W.M. Hughes, the electrical engineer and contractor, who became Chief Officer of Kidderminster Fire Brigade.

This picture of the New Road premises of W.M. Hughes, the electrical engineer, was taken around 1900. Mr Hughes gained much of his experience in the employ of The National Telephone Company. He fitted Astley Hall, the home of three-time prime minister Stanley Baldwin, with more than 200 electric lights. At the start of the twentieth century he performed the majority of the fitting for The Kidderminster and District Electric Lighting Traction Company. In his attractive showroom there was every kind of fitting imaginable for electrical items such as lights, bells and alarms. The adjoining workshops were mainly used for repairing goods and preparing new orders. A large proportion of the work involved nickel plating but Mr Hughes' speciality was the supply of electric motors to factories for the driving of looms and machinery. He could foresee the time when these would replace steam and gas.

J. Sanders was the manager of the Kidderminster Cycle Company that was established in 1891. Later he owned the Royal Severn cycle depot situated at 58 New Road, on the left-hand corner of Corporation Street. He was an agent for Sunbeam, Singer, Star and Triumph cycles, the Mabley motor car and the Excelsior motorcycle, and the maker of the Royal Severn cycle which had a very successful racing record. The business also bought and sold cars, stocked petrol and motor parts and charged accumulators. The Kidderminster Cycle Company was eventually wound up, unable to compete with the Birmingham and Coventry manufacturers.

An advertisement from 1925. It is ironic that J. Sanders eventually ended up selling Raleigh cycles as it was one of the companies with whom the Kidderminster Cycle Company could not compete. Certainly a case of 'if you can't beat 'em, join 'em'.

The Really Cheapest Bicycle for Everybody is the

RALEIGH

THE ALL-STEEL BICYCLE

Cheapness consists in the complete cost of an article. The first cost may be low, but if the bicycle is constantly in the repair shop the cost soon mounts up, to say nothing of the lost pleasure of riding. A Raleigh never needs repairs and is always ready to give the best service to its rider. That the output of the Raleigh factory has now reached 120,000 bicycles a

First Workman—"I'd like a Raleigh, but I can't afford it."
Second Workman—"My dear chap, you'll save its cost in a year."
First Workman—"But I can't raise the cash for it just now."
Second Workman—"Pay for it as you go, out of 'bus and tram fares saved. That's how I got mine. And don't forget that a Raleigh costs practically nothing to run and never a penny in repairs."

Send a postcard for "The Book of the Raleigh."

year shows how the public appreciates the fact. Every Raleigh is Guaranteed for Ever—not just for any limited period. It will last its rider's lifetime. Easy to learn it is comfortable and easy to ride, because of its superb construction and many special features. You will find all about these in "The Book of the Raleigh," free by post.

J. SANDERS,
58, New Road,
KIDDERMINSTER.

Tel. 209.

The Raleigh is built entirely of the finest cold-rolled steel (no malleable iron castings as in other bicycles), and is by far the cheapest bicycle in the end.

From £7 : 12 : 6 or by easy payments from 10/6 monthly

With Dunlop tyres and Sturmey-Archer 3 speed gear a Raleigh makes cycling a joy, as well as saving the pocket all the time. You only know what real cycling is when you ride a Raleigh.

The Kidderminster Cycle Club at the Bay Horse, Market Street, *c.* 1894.

The cattle market entrance in New Road. The first market was held here on 26 October 1871, but previously the market had been held in the streets, particularly Mill Street, High Street and Worcester Street. Horses were still sold, as they had been for centuries, in the Horsefair.

There were always plenty of cattle...

…sheep…

…pigs…

…and cars.

Work began on a new cattle market at an eight acre site at the top of Comberton Hill in June 1955 and was opened on 8 September 1959. It closed in 1998, mainly due to the drop in business caused by the BSE epidemic.

Market Street in 1971.

The entrance to Pike Mills, New Road, in the 1950s.

The School of Science & Art and the Free Library in the early twentieth century. The land for the site was donated by D.W. Goodwin.

The general Post Office.

The demolition of the School of Science & Art and the Free Library.

An aerial view of Kidderminster, *c.* 1930. Comberton Hill is at the bottom of the photograph. Bromsgrove Street is on the left with the Playhouse next to it and second left is Anchorfields. The third road from the left is George Street with New church on the left-hand corner and Laughton Goodwin's garage a short distance further up on the right-hand side. At the top, in the middle, St George's church can be seen and in the top right is St Ambrose's.

Bromsgrove Street with its early nineteenth-century factory workers' houses, *c.* 1952. Half of this street disappeared with the development of the ring road.

Mrs Elizabeth Braginton's greengrocers at 27 Comberton Hill was listed in *Kelly's Business Directory* in 1884 and 1904.

The Playhouse

Telephone: Kidderminster 3760

'Commencing Boxing Day

AGENCIA Productions Proudly Present

"ALADDIN"

A family pantomime for young and old with

JEAN ANN PAGE, LARRY GRAYSON, MARILYN CARROLL, THE DARRELL BROTHERS, THE AGENCIA YOUNG LADIES, THE CRAIGMORE BABES and

LARRY MARSH

Admission 3/-, 5/- and 6/6. Reduced Rates for Adult Parties. Children and Pensioners 2/6, 4/- and 6/6 (Except Saturday Evenings) : All Seats are Bookable.

December 26th, 28th, 29th, 30th, 31st, January 1st, 4th, 5th, 6th, 11th and 14th at 2.30 p.m. and 7.30 p.m.

January 2nd, 9th and 16th at 2.0, 5.0 and 8.0 p.m.

January 7th, 8th, 12th, 13th and 15th at 7.30 p.m. only

BOOK NOW

A wooden Theatre Royal was opened in 1891 and the first moving pictures seen in Kidderminster were shown here in 1896, between live shows. The theatre was replaced by the Opera House in 1903 and then reopened in 1946 as the Playhouse. This was closed in 1968 with the development of the ring road.

An advertisement from the *Shuttle* for the 1964 pantomime with Larry Grayson, before he was a household name.

Just below the Opera House was Worcester Cross. The cross took its name from the medieval Worcester Cross that marked the boundary of the town and stood where the Brinton drinking fountain is today. This was a busy area of the town with buildings that were very similar in appearance to those still remaining in the Horsefair.

The same scene in 1985. The area has been greatly changed by the construction of the ring road.

J.P. Harvey & Co. had extensive premises in Oxford Street.

The business of J.P. Harvey was established in 1860 in Oxford Street, opposite where the Central Cinema was later built. The business was started on a small scale because only a limited amount of capital was available. Deliveries were made on a single cart hauled by a donkey to customers from a small district. The very spacious premises in Oxford Street stretched back to Worcester Street and this allowed a large amount of material to be stored.

The business was confined to the sale of corn, seeds and manure until the company purchased the flour mill in Mill Street that was previously operated by Minifie and Son. This was a steam driven mill with premises that were equipped with the machinery for crushing and grinding corn and other feed. The firm had a large warehouse at the GWR station on Comberton Hill, where railway trucks ran alongside for loading and unloading, and a branch depot at Brierley Hill. The flour mill was altered after its acquisition by the installation of a complete roller plant and the erection of a large warehouse adjoined to the mill. The weekly output was about 1,000 sacks of flour as well as a large quantity of meal and feed.

From humble beginnings the company had progressed from a cart pulled by a donkey to twenty horses hauling wagons that delivered their products throughout a significant section of the Midlands. As the mill was located on the canal, a large proportion of the grain was received by barge. The canal also provided excellent shipping facilities as they were still extensively used in the early twentieth century when the members of the firm were Josiah Harvey and S. Harvey Loynes.

Another feature of the firm was the preparation of a variety of manures for particular soil or crops, which were the result of many years of experimenting. By the start of the twentieth century the intelligent use of manures had become a science, as the marketable value of the crop depended largely on the nature of the fertilizer applied to the soil.

(This discription has been adapted from the *Kidderminster Shuttle*, Industrial Number, *c.* 1903.)

Harvey's Mill, Mill Street, shortly before its demolition in 1976.

The Central Cinema just after its closure, c. 1985. It was opened on 5 October 1931 and was the finest of Kidderminster's picture houses.

The Central Cinema during its demolition in 1985.

Watkins' The White Shop was situated in New Road at the junction with Oxford Street. The sign above the shop illustrates what a wide range of services were provided.

This view of the site in 1999 shows that it is now occupied by Lawrences Pine Centre.

T. Crisp's tobacco and fishing tackle store at 19 Oxford Street was established around 1890 (above left). The shop kept a good stock of walking sticks and smokers' requisites of every description, and also contained a comprehensive fishing tackle department. Mr Crisp, being an ardent angler, was always ready to give his advice to other participants of the sport. Later, the shop was run by F. Oseland (above right). The same building still remains largely unchanged in 1998 (left). Does all that writing still exist under the paint work?

A Tyler, Hall & Co. window display from the 1920s. In 1925 two brothers from Dudley, Wilf and Frank Tyler, purchased the tenancy of a small shop in Oxford Street and set up in business as a men's outfitters, under the name of Tyler Brothers. The premises were originally erected as a tram shelter as this was the terminus for the trams which ran to Stourport and Comberton. In 1936 Frank took over sole ownership of the business and traded under the name of Frank H. Tyler until his death in 1951. He was joined by his son in 1946 who continued to run the business with his wife Betty. In 1969 they took over Hall and Co., an established men's outfitters in Stourbridge, and traded from both shops under the new name of Tyler, Hall and Co. They were joined by their son Jim in the middle of the 1970s and celebrated fifty years in business in June 1975.

Hodge & Hand, Oxford Street, 1999. Reginald Hodge, a native of Kidderminster, started his tailoring business at Market Chambers, 98 Coventry Street, around 1923. The business remained there for a number of years before moving to 27 Park Butts and is shown at that address in the 1940 edition of *Kelly's Business Directory*. In the early 1950s a partnership was set up with Fred Hand and the business was moved to its current Oxford Street site. Mr Hand left the business after a few years for unknown reasons. When Mr Hodge passed away in 1972 the business passed on to his daughter, Miss Jose Hodge, who had been working with her father since about 1956. She carries on the tradition of selling good quality menswear with which the name has become synonymous for over seventy-five years.

Thomas H. Hunter's tobacconist shop in Oxford Street.

Mr Fred Taylor, who occupied the premises prior to Tommy Hunter, ran a tobacconist shop that supplied the retail and wholesale trade and opened in 1877. It consisted of smart, modern premises that always showed an attractive display of novelties in the window. The interior was packed with supplies that included various kinds of loose and packet tobaccos, pipes, pouches, cigar and cigarette tubes, tobacco jars and snuffboxes. Mr Taylor also sold his own mixtures. One of the most popular was Taylor's celebrated 'Bobby's Mixture' made from selected sun-dried American tobaccos and, it is said, one of the finest and most economical mixtures available, selling at $3\frac{1}{2}$d per ounce, with Taylor's Irish Twist selling at 2d and 3d per ounce.

The wholesale side of the business supplied licensed victuallers and small retailers in the area. There were especially low terms quoted for larger orders. After forty-one years the business was sold to Thomas Hunter in 1918 and set up as a wholesale and retail tobacconist with the shop at the front and storage space at the rear. At this time Mr Hunter was the landlord of the Cape of Good Hope and had also been a professional footballer with Wolverhampton Wanderers FC. In a FA Cup match in the 1886/87 season he scored five goals in the 14-0 defeat of Crosswell's Brewery. They were knocked out by Aston Villa in the next round after four very arduous matches. Tommy played in the 1889 FA Cup Final when Wolves were defeated 3-0 by Preston North End in front of 22,250 spectators at the Oval, a record attendance for the time. Tragically, Mr and Mrs Hunter died on the same day in late October 1918, victims of the great flu epidemic which swept the country and actually claimed more victims than the bubonic plague.

In 1919 Arthur, Thomas' younger son, came out of the army and took over the business, running it for fifty years before handing over control to John K. Hunter who had been with the company since 1947. At the beginning of the 1980s, John's sons Richard and Paul joined the business. Expansion had taken place on the wholesale side and they supplied businesses within the West Midlands area.

The shop is one of the few remaining specialist tobacconists in the West Midlands carrying a wide range of pipe tobaccos, imported cigarettes, Havana cigars and other smokers' requisites.

Tommy Hunter played footnall for Wolves FC. Here he is, front row, extreme left, *c.* 1886.

The interior of Hunter's shop, in 1999.

Harry E. James, a hatter and hosier at 63 Oxford Street was listed in *Kelly's Directory* for 1904 and 1912.

Oxford Street in the 1920s. The Co-op buildings are on the left and the Green Man & Still public house is the second building on the right.

Two
Retail Market to Worcester Street

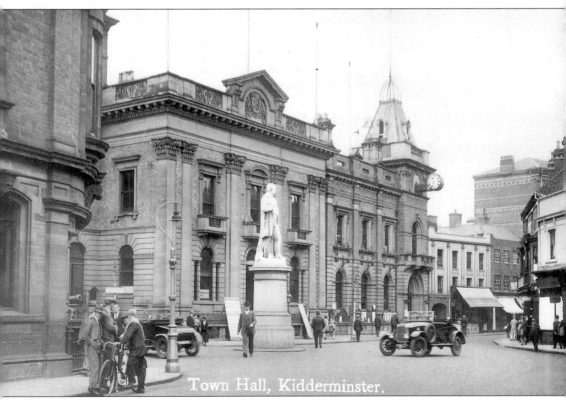

Town Hall, Kidderminster.

The hall, which opened on 19 January 1877, cost £8,000 and was built to the plans of J.T. Meredith. The statue to Sir Rowland Hill was erected in 1881, two years after his death. He is buried in Westminster Abbey.

Looking from inside Retail Market towards Oxford Street. Stalls were set up on the pavement at the bottom of the market steps. In the middle background the Green Man & Still can be seen.

The market entrance, looking from Oxford Street. The old Retail Market had stood on this site since 1822 and attracted people from far and wide, especially the Black Country. If the market that was held in Market Street is included, it is difficult to think of many items that could not be purchased in Kidderminster. The Market Hall was closed on 30 March 1974 and has been greatly missed by the people who remember it.

Inside the Market Hall there was always plenty of fresh fruit and vegetables on display.

The High Street end of the Retail Market.

The High Street entrance. W.H. Taylor had a confectionery stall at the entrance to the High Street end and was there for many years. The business was established in 1896 as a yeast merchant, a manufacturing confectioner and a supplier of sundries to bakers. In 1911 W.H. Taylor joined Colders Yeast Company Ltd. He retained the confectionery business to make a variety of boiled drops from cane sugar. Glucose, syrup or other cheapening materials were not used so that the highest standard of purity was maintained in all his sweets. His cough drops were recommended for young and old alike. The stall was stocked with a wide range of chocolates and all customers were assured of civility and attention to their business.

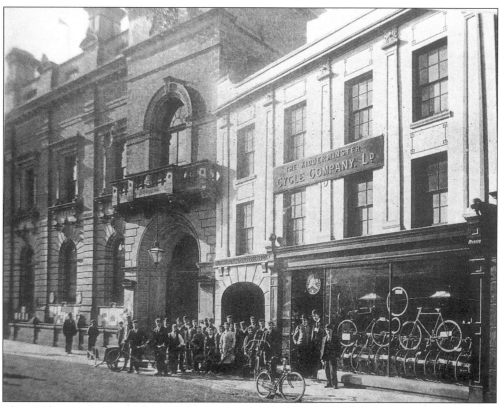

The Kidderminster Cycle Company's premises in Vicar Street, *c.* 1900 (see p. 22).

(see p. 22)

Simpson & Son, *c.* 1908. The Simpsons' shop was established in 1790 and could be found in Vicar Street for many years. They occupied the premises where the Kidderminster Cycle Company had previously operated. The premises were occupied by Mac Fisheries in the 1950s and Mothercare by 1998.

One of Simpson's vans can be seen on the left of this view of Vicar Street in the early 1950s.

W.L. Quick the tailor and jeweller had a shop in Vicar Street, opposite the Town Hall.

E.F. Allen & Sons sold pianos and organs from their shop in Vicar Street. The business was established in 1840 by Mr E.F. Allen and the head office was in Wolverhampton. After his death the business passed to his sons who displayed enterprise by opening branches in Cannock, Stafford, West Bromwich, Shrewsbury and Birmingham. Declining to handle inferior goods, the name of Allen gradually became synonymous with high quality pianos and moderate and easy terms of business. In 1900 the company extended its operations to Kidderminster when it purchased the business of the late Mr Jackson at 6 Vicar Street, which was situated about halfway along the road, next to the entrance to the Retail Market. They entirely renovated the shop by trebling its former capacity and putting in large windows. This made it one of the most attractive shops in town. In later years the business moved to Tower Buildings, Blackwell Street. In the late 1950s the shop passed to Willsons who sold organs, guitars and records.

Joseph Sanders was a boot and shoe factor at 7 Vicar Street, c. 1900. The establishment did a strictly cash trade in boots and shoes and was taken over by Mr Sanders in the latter part of the nineteenth century. The shoe shop had a good frontage and interior with a large storeroom on the first floor. Mr Sanders purchased his wares from the leading manufacturers and carried a large number of popular lines which were recommended for quality material, smart style and reliable workmanship. His prices were amongst the keenest in the area. Mr Sanders was also well known as a cycle manufacturer and agent with a shop in New Road and as the manager of the Kidderminster Cycle Company (see p. 22). A busy man indeed!

PC Dick Hill was the last member of the old Kidderminster Police Force and was allowed to keep the spike on his helmet. He is pictured here with Sir George Eddy shortly before the police box at the bottom of High Street was dug up.

Morgan & Lawley's pharmacy and opticians was at 14 and later 16 Vicar Street. It is listed in *Kelly's Directory* from 1884 until 1928.

Craddock Bros had a shoe shop in the Bull Ring in the late nineteenth century which was later occupied by Fosters Jewellers. They then moved across the Bull Ring, next to the Medical Hall, and owned a shop at the bottom of High Street.

Craddocks in 1968, just prior to the demolition that made room for the Swan Centre.

A particularly early photograph of Attwood and Isaac's store.

One of the earliest records for a shop on this site dates back to 1840 when the store belonged to R.B. Belcher & Co. Their combination of running a wholesale and retail linen and woollen drapers and a complete funeral business was an unusual one. R.J. Ransome, formerly of John Evans of Birmingham, followed Belcher's before the store was acquired by the brothers George and Charles Isaac. The premises became known as Regent House and the Isaacs traded as tailors, hatters, outfitters, drapers and milliners.

At the turn of the century millinery was produced and more than a dozen milliners were employed in rooms that later became offices. Some staff lived on the premises: the apprentices mainly occupied the attic rooms with a housekeeper to maintain good behaviour. Travelling tailors would also live on the premises and were housed in the old stables at the bottom of the yard where the late R.J. Ransome had kept his carriage and pair. A business around the turn of the twentieth century of this size would have been quite an operation to run, but would certainly have had its advantages for the employer.

In 1877 Mr Harry Attwood was an apprentice to the Isaacs and when George retired Mr Attwood became the manager of the business. After Charles Isaac also called it a day and retired to the south of England, Mr Attwood, who now owned the business, went into partnership with Robert Isaac who had also been an apprentice with the firm. During this time the Isaacs and Mr Ransome had lived on the premises.

When he retired, Harry Attwood turned the business into a private company. After his death in 1939, his widow Ethel ran the business with Edgar Wallis as the manager until it was sold to Great Universal Stores.

There is some speculation that the store could have been the original site of the Lion Hotel as there was, at one time, a lion's head above the Trinity Lane entrance and a reclining lion above the archway leading to the lawn at the rear of the premises. The cellars may also have been constructed to allow the storage of barrels. Many of the cellar ceiling beams were old ship timbers and were notched and numbered for the wooden ribs.

At present, T.J. Hughes is one of Kidderminster's more versatile and popular shops, largely due to their large and varied stock and their competitive prices. Prior to T.J. Hughes the store was owned by Hamilton and Bell and Owen-Owen.

W. Pritchard was at the bottom of High Street on the right-hand side. Albert and William Pritchard moved to Kidderminster in the early 1900s and Albert established a drapery business at 2 High Street in 1908. Within two or three years the business moved to 26 High Street. William took over the business around 1924 when Albert moved to Tenbury Wells to establish a drapery business in Market Street. Meanwhile, the business in High Street had been extended to include 25 High Street. In 1929 Montague Burton took over the premises and built a new shop on the site while William moved his business to 9 High Street.

Pritchard, 9 High Street, *c.* 1930.

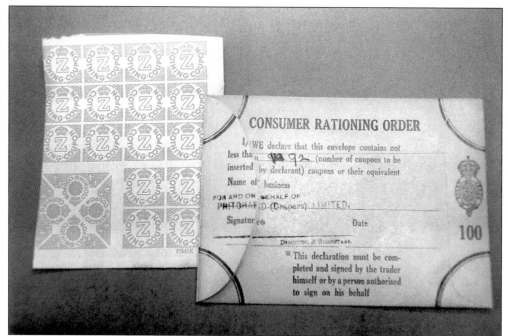

Clothing coupons from the Second World War for Pritchard.

Pritchard, Oxford Street, 1999. At present the business is at 22/23 Oxford Street after it moved there in the middle of the 1960s to make way for the redevelopment of the town centre. This redevelopment involved High Street and Swan Street; the last building between the two was demolished in 1968. The business is now run by William Pritchard's grandson, Tony Chambers, who started in the business in 1948. He is assisted by his wife Sheila and two sons Peter and Russell.

An advertisement from the *Kidderminster Shuttle*, c. 1925. Corsets were obviously the order of the day as women became more fashion conscious in the roaring twenties.

CORSETS

Twilfit Corsets give perfect freedom of movement and adequate support and have proved themselves to be the Best Corset Value in the World ; they are the only corsets carrying a full guarantee against everything.

Model 77.
A charming low bust model, fitted with rustle and unbreakable "Twilfit Spiral" Steels and four strong hose supporters. In Pink. **8/5**

Model Sports A.
Made with elastic round top, specially adapted for slender figures. In pink and white. Fitted with rustless and unbreakable "Twilfit-Spiral" Steels and four hose supporters. **4/11**

MODEL 141.
Corselet of handsome broche. Specially suitable for sports or for full figures if worn over Corsets. It will greatly assist in moulding the figure to good proportions. In pink and white. Bust size, 30-42 ins. PRICE **12/9**

Every Twilfit Corset is fitted with rustless and unbreakable Spiral Steels, an exclusive Twilfit feature.

Twilfit Corsets carry a definite guarantee of "Money returned or corsets exchanged if not completely satisfied."

MANY OTHER MODELS ALSO IN STOCK.
SEE OUR DISPLAY.

Model Sports 3.
Strong elastic round top. In pink and white. fitted with rustless and unbreakable "Twilfit Spiral" Steels and four strong hose supporters. **9/6**

Model 2003.
A sports model for slender figures, in white only. Silk elastic at top, lightly boned with "Twilfit Spiral" Steels and fitted with four strong hose supporters. **10/6**

WILLIAM PRITCHARD,
25-26, HIGH STREET and VICAR STREET, **Kidderminster.** Tel. **326.**

55

Andrews, the ladies' outfitters, could be found at 23 High Street.

Andrews, LADIES' OUTFITTERS
23, High St., Kidderminster

The cabbies' shelter, High Street, c. 1900. The cabmen's shelter was a gift from Mr John Brinton in 1878. It stood at the bottom left-hand side of High Street on the former site of the guildhall. This was only intended as a temporary site as there had been many objections to the area being used as a stand for cabs. The shelter was a refuge for the cabbies to enable them to rest, keep warm and have a place to eat their food. It was suggested that the cabbies make a subscription of two (old) pence per week to help maintain the shelter.

A cabbie in High Street in the late nineteenth century.

The cabbie's shelter in Brinton Park in 1985. The shelter from High Street ended its days in Brinton Park where it was used to store bowls for the bowling green. Unfortunately, it was vandalised in the 1990s and, as a result, it was demolished.

W. Copeland, 6 High Street, was a goldsmith, jeweller, watchmaker and optician. W. Copeland learnt his trade in Coventry and set up his business around 1873. He specialised in watches and a large part of his shop was given to an extensive stock of watches of all descriptions. These were difficult to match for quality, style and cheapness, whether it was a moderately priced silver watch or the costliest gold hunter on the market. W. Copeland also specialised in repairing clocks of every description on his premises. Watches and clocks were only a part of his business, however, as he stocked a wonderful array of high-class jewellery and was also an optician.

The interior of Copeland's shop.

A 1910 view showing the premises of Mrs W. Randle Cooper, a cook and confectioner at Baxter House, High Street. The business was founded around 1850 and enjoyed an excellent reputation for supplying superior goods at moderate prices. After taking control around 1900, Mrs Cooper continued in the same vein. Before coming to Kidderminster, she gained considerable experience in a number of places including Cambridge. Her specialities were cakes for weddings and christenings, raised pies, ices, jellies, creams and soups. Mrs Cooper was also noted for her excellent curd cheese cakes, tarts and pastry. The goods were prepared daily from the finest ingredients and in many instances the recipes were unique to the establishment, resulting in the stock being as wholesome and pleasing to the palate as they were tempting to the eye. The building was the birthplace of the Revd Richard Baxter and was named after him. After the frontage and interior had been re-modelled and decorated in a manner that was suited to the period, it was seen as one of the most appealing confectioners in town. In addition to the sales department on the ground floor, the accommodation included an elegantly furnished dining room and refreshment rooms where luncheon, dinner and afternoon tea was served. A wine and beer licence was also held.

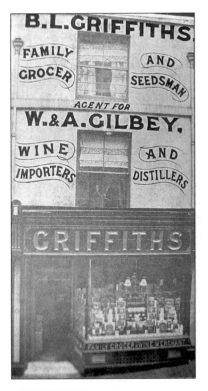

At the rear of High Street was Swan Street and at No. 6 was Mr B.L. Griffiths a grocer, tea dealer, seedsman and cheese, butter and bacon factor. The business was founded in 1833 and acquired by Mr Griffiths around 1890. By the early twentieth century this was one of the oldest and most established businesses of its type in Kidderminster. The window displayed a wide selection of high-class groceries while on the right of the entrance was a long range of counters that extended the entire length of the shop. Two handsome glass cases were seated on part of the counters and contained toilet soaps, chocolates and high-class confectionery, and a third case was dedicated to candied fruits and associated goods. Behind the counter elegant fixtures displayed ornate canisters of tea, bottled pickles, sauces and preserved goods from Crosse and Blackwell and other celebrated manufacturers. The end of the shop was mainly devoted to English provisions including ham, bacon and cheese. Garden seeds and Gilbey's wines were also sold. Mr Griffiths was a keen cyclist and one of the first people to ride a 'Safety' in Kidderminster. A number of rounds were set up for the prompt delivery of orders in and around Kidderminster and there were also rounds every four weeks to Chaddesley, Bewdley, Blakedown, Cookley and Wolverley.

Meredith Bros were situated at 20 High Street. As well as being a large general grocer's, they also had an extensive china and fancy goods department on the first floor. They are listed in *Kelly's Directory* from 1884 to 1916. The site is now occupied by Marks & Spencer.

The cashier's office at Meredith Bros.

The grocery and meat department could be found on the ground floor.

The china and fancy department was situated on the first floor.

This view of J. Fehrenbach & Son, the high-class confectioners on High Street, was taken around 1903. The business was originally situated in Bridge Street before it moved to Coventry Street after about six years. The business then moved to the premises in the photograph, at the top right-hand side of High Street. J. Fehrenbach & Son was one of the leading bakers and confectioners in Kidderminster and their tearooms were one of the most frequently visited places in the town: it was attended by visitors from near and far. The shop was fitted in a luxurious style with a mahogany counter and fittings and elegant furniture and drapery, which combined to convey the impression that no money had been spared to achieve sheer elegance and comfort. The three tearooms were furnished in an equally elegant style that was in keeping with the intention of the firm to have an establishment that should be second to none.

Noah's Ark, 61 Worcester Street, *c*. 1902.
Noah's Ark was established in its Worcester
Street location around 1862 and was acquired
by Miss Florence E. Basford about 1896. Under
her control things soon began to change: the
upstairs showroom was abandoned and the shop
on the ground floor increased to six times its
original size. This allowed the owner to create a
bazaar with hundreds of toys and knick-knacks
temptingly displayed on shelves and tables
throughout the roomy premises. There was also
an extensive toy and general bazaar upstairs and
the whole place was simply packed with goods.
Customers could walk round, inspect at their
leisure and buy at their pleasure. Six staff were
usually employed but this increased to twelve at
Christmas. The establishment was invariably
worth a visit as it always contained something
new and attractive, and was held in high esteem
by young and old alike. It was often included in
the shopping itinerary of many of the wealthy
families connected with the district. With
Kidderminster the centre of a splendid fishing
district, Miss Basford also specialised in keeping
everything required by the angler.

The shop was burnt out in 1907 and the
premises unfortunately suffered such damage
that it did not reopen.

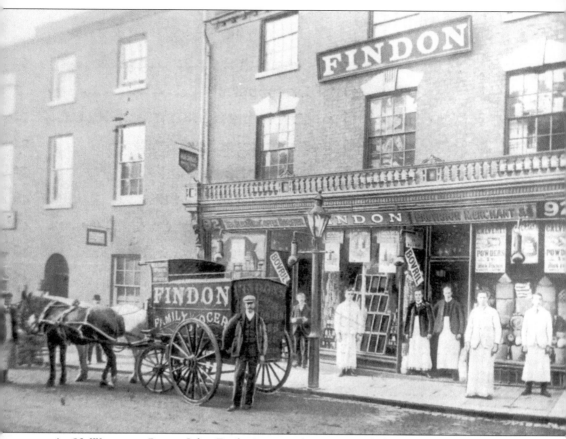

At 92 Worcester Street, John Findon's many functions included being a tea blender, coffee roaster, family grocer, provision dealer and a wine, spirit and beer merchant.

John Findon was one of the leading suppliers of groceries and provisions in the area. The business was founded by his father Alderman John Findon in the middle of the nineteenth century and on his death passed to his two sons who carried on the business as J. & A. Findon.

The partnership was dissolved in 1896 by mutual consent when Alfred became the proprietor of a large coal haulage business which the firm had built up over a period of time. John Findon became the sole owner of the grocery business, which could be compared to a type of early Sainsbury's store. John had a thorough knowledge of each department and created a thriving business by supplying other grocers as well as the general public.

The premises in Worcester Street comprised of a large shop with three spacious windows, two entrances and a frontage that was about fifty feet wide. The interior contained a provision section with marble top counters, smart cases, stands and fittings. At the rear there were capacious basement cellars, large stores and a warehouse. Agencies were held for the famous Mazawattee, Ridgeway and Tower teas as well as Mr Findon's own blends of choice Indian and Ceylon teas that were all at reasonable prices. Another notable feature of the house was the coffee. The coffee beans were young but well matured before they were ground and roasted at frequent intervals during the week. Upon entering the premises a vast number of aromas must have attacked your senses as, in addition to the tea blending and coffee roasting, chocolate, cocoa, spices and dessert fruits could also be found. Rooms were specially constructed for drying and storing hams and bacon. The basement was used for storing dried fruits and also contained machinery for washing and drying the fruit.

The shop interior, showing the tea, coffee and provisions department.

The bottling cellar for John Findon's business.

The yard at the rear of John Findon's premises.

Looking up Worcester Street. Findon's is on the left with the car parked outside.

Three
Park Butts to Clensmore

The arrival of the canals in the second half of the eighteenth century gave the carpet factories access to the UK and seaports around the world. This shows the canal where it passed under Mill Street. The building on the right is the rear of the Black Horse Hotel. This is unrecognisable today.

Roland Onslow, greengrocer and fishmonger, Park Butts. There had been an Onslow shop on the Butts for a long time until it was destroyed to make way for the ring road in the 1960s. The shop was in a prime position to catch potential customers as they walked into town. Where have all the people gone?

Barry Onslow was the last member of the family to run a green grocer's business, until he retired from this line of work in 1969. Born in Kidderminster at 8 Crane Street in 1933 he started school in 1938 at Bennett Street before moving to New Meeting aged seven and Harry Cheshire at eleven. When he was around nine-years-old, Barry started to help in the shop. On Saturdays, mainly he served customers and provided general assistance. Produce was purchased from Birmingham, but in 1942 the Onslows were only able to make the trip once a week due to the petrol rationing, unless Mrs Onslow could beg one or two coupons from a kind customer. A particularly good source was a gentleman who owned a garage in Cleobury Mortimer. Barry would travel with his father Roland to arrive in Birmingham at 4.00 a.m. and get back to the shop by 7.30, before he went to school for 9.00 a.m. It was amazing how he managed to stay awake! After the war and petrol rationing, Birmingham Market was visited five and perhaps six times per week, while the shop would sometimes stay open until 11.00 p.m. on Fridays and Saturdays.

Barry worked in the shop full time from 1948, when he was aged fifteen, until 1969. He then left the family firm, purchased Beard's television shop in Lombard Street, Stourport, and set up his own business with his wife Jill. The business was built up over two years before the decision was made to sell. After the deal was all but settled the new owner realised that he needed a lorry but could not afford to buy one. Barry reckoned his lorry, which he was now selling, was worth a £1,000, so he suggested that the matter was settled by the spin of a coin. Double or quits, £2,000 or the lorry. Unfortunately, Barry lost.

As Barry had not been on holiday for more than twenty years he decided that he would see the world with his wife and two children. Over the next 6 months he travelled 22,000 miles in a Ford Transit van through much of continental Europe, the Middle East and Africa. Some of the Onslow's memorable adventures included travelling on Mousel roads that were so bad that it took 6 days to travel 130 miles and travelling 6 hours in second gear in the Atlas Mountains. The fact that the van did not require any spares was a credit to the Ford Transit.

Prior to embarking on their trip, a shop had been purchased in the Horsefair, at the bottom of Hurcott Road. It was refurbished over the next few months and opened in February 1973. The business was an instant success and at weekends employed up to twelve staff. They stayed there for two years before deciding to sell. Nevertheless, Barry still supplied produce to fish and chips shops from Birmingham to Malvern with Bob Matthews, who assisted him between 1975 and 1982. In 1982 Barry decided to retire from business completely. It was not long, however, before he was running another shop in Worcester Street. The lease was eventually purchased in conjunction with his new partner Fred Hewlett. He sold the business after six successful years and once again retired.

One last story is typical of Barry Onslow. As Easter 1963 approached, Barry bet two of his friends, Cedric Grainger the butcher and Trevor Roberts the turf accountant, £50 that he could not make it to Monte Carlo and back in four days. A £5 note was torn in half with one half being kept by Trevor Roberts and the other to be sent back from Monte Carlo as proof. Barry set off on Easter Sunday morning in his TR3, spent 25 minutes in Monte Carlo and returned by Monday night. He covered 2,000 miles and spent £52.

Thus ends a brief but colourful recollection of one Kidderminster shopkeeper's exploits. Do not be surprised if you suddenly see a shop opening up with the name Barry Onslow on it!

The unique Barry Onslow.

The remains of Onslow's shop, shortly before the construction of the ring road.

Charlie Brown was born in Kidderminster in 1891. His father was a hairdresser in George Street, opposite the Golden Lion. Charlie left school at fourteen and worked in a cycle shop in Worcester Street for two years before he left to work for the newly opened Castle Motor Company as an apprentice engineer. Due to poor health, the family doctor suggested that he should work outdoors and after passing his RAC driving test in 1910 (which cost him 25p), he worked as a chauffeur with the Castle Motor Company. By 1914 Charlie had become manager at the Vicar Street showroom. His natural flair as a salesman meant that the company's agency for B.S.A. Motorcycles was very successful. Charlie was also given the job of exhibiting the Castle-Three at the Olympia Motor Cycle Show, where a large number of orders were received. Charlie had a particularly good rapport with Sir Herbert Smith when he owned the Vicar Street shop as they were both such outspoken individuals. Charlie left Castle in 1928 to manage Butts Motor Depot, which was owned by Stanley Goodwin, where he sold petrol and cars. Charlie did not like dealing with part-exchange vehicles and gradually turned the business towards sports equipment, radios, toys and cameras. He convinced Stanley Goodwin that this would be more profitable and was eventually proved right. Charlie remained for thirty-three years before retiring in 1961, aged seventy. He passed away in 1975 aged eighty-four.

An advertisement from the *Shuttle*, 1919.

Motor Cycle Show, Olympia,
NOV. 24th to 29th, 1919.

WE ARE SHOWING THE

CASTLE THREE RUNABOUT.

THE PIONEER 3-wheeler, to adopt four-cylinder engine and shaft drive.

STAND No. 37.

WE ARE AGENTS FOR THE FOLLOWING MOTOR CYCLES :—

B.S.A.	Humber	Royal Enfield	Viper Jap
Clyno	Levis	A.B.C	Rover
	Alldays Allon	Bat, etc.	

Side-Cars : Canolet, Klassic, etc.

A.B.C. SKOOTAMOTO. SIMPLEX, Attachment for Cycles
"EVENRUDE" ROW BOAT MOTOR.

WRITE OR WIRE US—**STAND No. 37.**
OUR SALESMEN will be in attendance, and at your service.

The Castle Motor Co., Ltd.
KIDDERMINSTER.

The Butts Motor Depot, *c.* 1935.

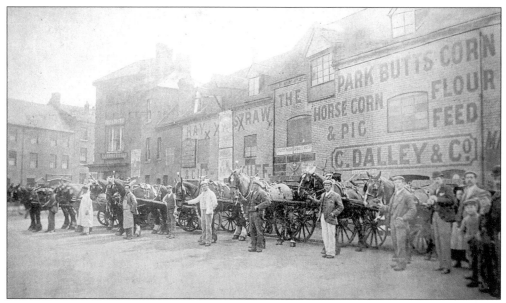

Clement Dalley & Co., agricultural produce exchange, Park Butts, *c.* 1900.

In Park Butts there are a number of venerable-looking buildings that bring back memories of people and events from the past. Butler Best, the first mayor of Kidderminster, ran a large and profitable business as a wool merchant and in the adjoining offices, James Chambers acted as agent for Danks, Venn and Saunders the Bridgwater Trustees. Crawley's, the great carting agents, ran a branch of their business from these buildings and Moses Whittall started here in a modest office until success drove him to more modern works. The Park Butts also witnessed the start of many other successful business ventures that used the canal which ran up to the premises as the principal means of communication and transport.

Clement Dalley commenced business in 1880 and made a successful effort to maintain the character of the historic premises, which were known among agriculturalists as being one of the busiest corners of Kidderminster. There was an emporium for all kinds of agricultural supplies and business was conducted on co-operative lines. During the transitional stage of agriculture when, due to continued pressure from foreign competition, farmers struggled to make ends meet, every effort was made to help them. They were given the best value for money as costs were cut to the minimum to ensure that they could be supplied with seeds, manures and feed.

In 1894 with agriculture still in an impoverished state, Clement Dalley began to investigate the possibility of sugar production from the growth of sugar beet. In 1898 trials were carried out at eleven farms for the growth of sugar beet. Of these, eight samples were of a higher purity than the 80 per cent required in the United States, while the overall average was 82.38 per cent. In 1905 a packed public meeting held at the Town Hall discussed the possibility of sugar production. Publicity continued over the next five years and on 23 August 1910 a large gathering of agricultural representatives met at the Town Hall to hear proposals on the construction of a sugar factory. The discussions continued over the next few years until the First World War intervened. It was not until 1925 that a factory was eventually built at Foley Park after parliament withdrew the tax on home produced sugar.

In later years, Dalley opened premises in New Road at the end of Market Street (known locally as Dalley's Corner) and on the new market site on Comberton Hill. They eventually joined forces with J.P. Harvey and the company became known as Harvey Dalley.

(This discription has been adapted from the *Kidderminster Shuttle*, Industrial Number, *c.* 1903.)

The Co-operative stores, around 1900, before they had been transformed into the Butts Depot.

Dalley's Corner, New Road, c. 1960.

The Butts entrance of Thompson & Parkes the builders, merchants and ironmongers. The firm was set up around 1937 by Eric Thompson and Colonel William Parkes at open-yard premises in Waterloo Street to supply the building trade. Eric Thompson, who had previously been employed by Timmis' ironmongers in Coventry Street, was the working partner while Colonel Parkes provided the finance. After moving to Charles Street, steady growth was made and around 1939 a property at 31 Mill Street was purchased because of the need for more space. In the early 1950s the firm acquired properties in Park Butts, again to allow for much needed expansion. The yard in Waterloo Street was later occupied by Mr Stubley, the scrap dealer. John and Richard Thompson joined the company in 1958 and in 1962 a site at Oldington Trading Estate was purchased. By 1976 the whole operation had been transferred to these premises. The company was sold in January 1999 but the trading name has been retained. John and Richard Thompson planned to retire from the firm in 1999.

Goodwin's Mill, Mill Street, *c.* 1902.

In 1086 when William the Conqueror produced the *Domesday Book,* a number of mills were shown on the survey for the area which is now Kidderminster and it is very likely that one or more of the mills were on the site of the Town Mills. John Doharty's map of 1753 shows the Town Mills with the watercourse arrangements just as they remained until quite recently. In 1809 the mill had five pairs of stones and it was insured for £900: £500 for the buildings and £400 for the waterwheel and machinery. The nineteenth-century millers were Benjamin Turrall (1820 and 1829), Thomas Turrall (1828 and 1835), John Turrall (1835 and 1841) and D.W. Goodwin (from the late 1850s).

Daniel Wagstaffe Goodwin was born at Holt in 1821 and died in 1890. The son of John G. Goodwin, the Alderman and Mayor of Worcester, he was a great benefactor to the town, donating the site for the Schools of Art and Science in Market Street and offering £500 toward the building of a new Free Library. He purchased the town flour mills in Mill Street in 1845 and largely rebuilt them. The building, built as a steam mill, remains today situated between the watermill and the road. It had four storeys and the date 1881 appears on the gable above the top storey.

In 1903 the watermill had 2 waterwheels that were around 12ft in diameter and could produce steam power of 160hp. It also had thirty wooden paddles surrounded by iron bar bracing, eight iron arms, an iron axle and a large pit wheel with teeth inside its rim. The ironwork was supplied by Turton's, which later became Bradley & Turton. By 1903 Goodwin & Co. had had a wharf on the canal for around 20 years and had linked it to the mill by a private tramway line that was about 290yds long. The introduction of automatic machinery led to the mill being regarded as one of the best in the district. The wheat fell through the hopper bottoms of the trucks and onto an elevator, before being carried to the top of the building where the first stage in the milling process started. The wheat passed through a series of cylindrical sieves to remove the impurities and was then washed and dried. It passed through a series of rollers, scalpers and purifiers before it was graded for sale. In sales presentations much was made of the fact that during the whole process the wheat was untouched by human hands.

(Part of this discription is reproduced by kind permission of Mr D.T.N. Booth, the former co-editor of Midland Wind & Water Mills Group.)

EVERY COOK can make good Cakes, Pastry, Etc.
but can MAKE BETTER by using—

Goodwin's "EXTRA"
Self-Raising FLOUR.

THE BEST BY FAR   GET IT AT YOUR GROCERS IN THE
Baby Picture Bag.

An advertisement from 1919 that shows the famous Goodwin's flour bag.

One of the waterwheels, revealed when the mill was demolished.

Grain being unloaded from the canal, c. 1902. St Mary's church is prominent in the background.

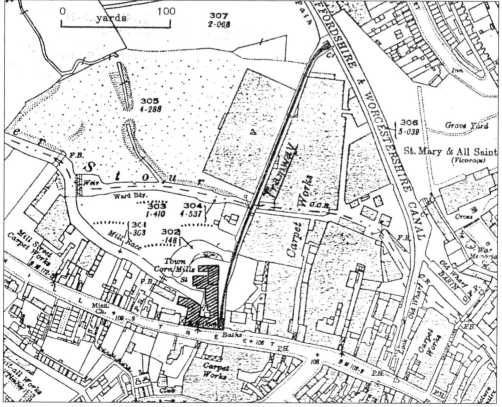

The location of the Town Mills, shown on a 25-inch Ordnance Survey map from 1924.

The rear view of the old steam mill premises, taken in 1999.

The Town Mills, 1999. The building that housed the steam mill was owned by the Motor Cycle Mart in the 1970s and 1980s but has recently been put up for sale.

This public fountain was donated by D.W. Goodwin and stood at Blakebrook. It was housed in this elegant building which here has an unknown lady seated in front of it.

The head offices of Carpet Trades Ltd, Mill Street, *c.* 1923. Carpet Trades was an amalgamation of established firms, comprising of James Humphries & Sons; Edward Hughes & Sons; Charles Harrison & Sons; Carpet Manufacturers, Kidderminster; Lea Ltd; Worsted Spinners, Kidderminster; Pyrah & Sons, Providence Mill, Heckmondwike; Robert Swire & Sons; Ravensthorpe Mills; Dewsbury Woollen Spinners. The company also had a felt manufacturing plant at Long Meadow Mills, Kidderminster. The extensive spinning mills in Yorkshire and Kidderminster supplied Kidderminster factories with raw materials for the manufacture of carpets. In the 1930s the company had 3,500 employees, over 600 looms and supplied goods throughout the world. They manufactured many types of carpet as well as certain special fabrics. These included the Anglo-Turkey carpet that was woven by machinery with the true Turkish knot. In later years, the company became known as Gilt Edge Carpets and then Coloroll, before it went out of business in the early 1990s. The factory was demolished in 1993.

Carpet Trades' offices in the 1950s.

Carpet Trades' carnival entry, *c.* 1927.

Carpet Trades celebrate the Coronation of George VI…

…can you find your grandmother?

The view from Carpet Trades' offices in January 1963, looking into Park Butts from Mill Street. During the winter of 1963 the town was in the grip of one of the worst winters on record. The construction of the ring road, however, later led to the disappearance of most things in this scene.

The sun sets on Coloroll at the commencement of demolition in 1993.

Staff of G. Hopkins & Son, the wine and spirit merchants, pose in front of their Mill Street premises. The firm were cider makers and wholesale bottlers of ales and stouts. The George public house had also been at this site since around 1793, but was closed in March 1968 for the ring road development.

Hopkins' Model Home Brewery, Greatfield Road, in 1999; the firm's name remains faintly on the wall. George Hopkins founded the business in 1859, developed it considerably and then passed it on to his son and former partner A.G. Hopkins in 1889. The firm's Mill Street headquarters consisted of offices and stores, extensive cellarage and a three-storey cider factory. The cellars were especially prepared to ensure efficient bottling and maturation. The well-selected stock included their celebrated White Wings whisky which was sold in two grades according to age, at forty-four shillings and forty-eight shillings per dozen bottles. The firm acted as the district's accredited bottlers for Allsopp, Bass, Worthington, Guinness and Jacobs Pilsner Lager Beer, while Burton ales and Guinness stout were supplied in casks. At the start of the twentieth century Hopkins' made a name for themselves as cider makers. The refreshing qualities of Worcestershire cider had long been recognised, but only in recent years has its manufacture had business potential. In the picking season tons of well-selected apples were ground, pressed and the juice passed by gravitation into suitable receivers to be fermented and racked from sediment as cider.

The first floor of the cider factory was principally used for storage, grinding and pressing.

The top floor of the cider factory was mainly used for storage and allowing the apples to mellow.

Mill Street, around 1900, with Hopkins' premises on the left.

Joseph Ray, the Alderman and Mayor of Kidderminster in 1917 and 1918, was a confectioner and baker on Station Hill. He came to Kidderminster from Huntingdon with his two brothers around 1886. Alfred set up a bakery in Wood Street that traded as Tony's Bread for many years and is now run by Joseph's great grandson, Steve Ray. James started a bakery in Stourbridge Road which later became Coalburns. His wife Sarah Emily (née Barnes) was a frequent speaker in various meetings held at Baxter church. She travelled widely in connection with missionary work visiting Australia, New Zealand, America and Canada. In the 1886 floods a wall collapsed in Joseph's Mill Street garden and he only saved himself by clinging onto a tree.

The exterior of Joseph Ray's shop at 26 Mill Street, c. 1905.

Some of the Kidderminster Master Bakers party at Lilleshall Hall on 4 July 1928. Back row, extreme left: Alfred Ray, the founder of the Wood Street Bakery.

S.F. Westwood, 86 Mill Street, *c.* 1905. Samuel F. Westwood was one of the many family grocers that could be found in the town around the turn of the century. By 1912 the business had moved to 3 Park Butts.

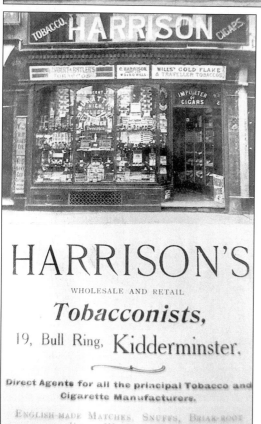

The business of Alex Kerr & Co. at 14 Mill Street was originally set up around 1840 and acquired by Alexander Kerr in about 1897. The success of the business was based on the reliable character of the goods rather than profuse advertising. There was a large and varied stock that included most articles found in a modern outfitter's shop at the time, from the moderately priced to the expensive. The speciality of the shop was to cater for the large class of customers for whom economy and elegance were of equal importance. Mr Kerr was assisted in the management of the business by Mr Alfred Woodward who had been associated with the establishment since 1857.

Harrison's wholesale and retail tobacconists, 19 Bull Ring, *c.* 1908.

T. Blunt, the Bull Ring, in the early twentieth century. For over 130 years Blunts Shoes have traded from the same premises in Kidderminster. While that alone is some achievement, one must also take into consideration that since its establishment, the River Stour has flooded at least fourteen times. The proximity of the building to the river might have made it difficult to acquire property insurance! Thomas Blunt (1841-1920) came to Kidderminster after completing his apprenticeship in Northampton and opened the Bull Ring shop in 1866 to make boots and shoes. He advertised in the first edition of the *Kidderminster Shuttle* on 12 February 1870. In the early years of the business, Thomas lived at the premises to save accommodation expenses, which he could probably have ill afforded while getting his venture off the ground. Thomas' elder sons were born and raised in these surroundings, so it was inevitable that they would follow their father into the business: Thomas Blunt jnr in 1900 and Harry in 1917. In 1957 two of Harry's sons, Tom and Bob, were made partners.

The Bull Ring, with Blunts on the left. The building being demolished housed a café below pavement level. In the 1960s a large part of the Bull Ring was demolished to make way for the new post office.

Holders, 5/6 Bull Ring, c. 1930. Mr C.F. Holder, the people's cash draper, is standing on the left while the gentleman on the right is probably Mr Minton who, in later years, was employed by Broadhurst Fabrics, Coventry Street. The earliest mention of these premises comes from 1745 when they formed part of the marriage settlement of William Arden of Birmingham. The business was founded by a Mr Roberts in 1832 and taken over by Mr Holder in the latter part of the nineteenth century. Mr Holder gained his business experience in Birmingham and soon made his mark in Kidderminster as a popular general draper, adept in the art of buying and catering for the large middle-class population of a manufacturing town. He made a strict rule of only supplying reliable goods and never allowed himself to be undersold, no matter what the cost. The trade which developed soon outgrew the premises and so No. 6 at the Bull Ring was acquired. It was transformed into a splendid, modern shop with features that included an entirely new front, a paved mosaic entrance, a looking-glass ceiling and a marble facia. Indeed, the shop may have been the first in Kidderminster to be illuminated by electric lighting. Nos 5 and 6 were both double-fronted with their own entrance. This allowed for plenty of window space for the display of general drapery, dresses and Manchester goods including Irish linens, fancy drapery, mantles, blouses, corsets and hosiery. The mantle showroom was upstairs and was one of the most special features of the establishment. Another speciality was the Manchester department that dealt with an immense stock of longcloths, calicoes, Irish linens, blankets, flannels and other fabrics of a similar type. The business was conducted on popular lines by a strict cash only basis.

A general view of the Bull Ring. The foreground is dominated by the statue of Richard Baxter.

Foster & Son with Holders next door in 1965, just prior to demolition. Blunts can be seen in the background.

Foster & Son had premises at 17 Bull Ring where they ran a practical watchmaking and jeweller's business.

Evan Foster started business in Kidderminster around 1869 having had considerable experience making levers for the escapement mechanism in watches. A wide choice of gold and silver English watches, gold jewellery, and electroplated items was kept. Estimates were given for re-silvering old plate and re-gilding jewellery as if it were new, and a service was also offered for winding clocks and keeping them repaired by the year.

Mr Foster had a son who was also named Evan and in the 1912 edition of the *Kelly's Business Directory* the firm was advertised as Foster and Son. By 1916 the business had moved to the other side of the Bull Ring to No. 3, the former premises of the boot manufacturers, the Craddock Brothers. As business improved further it was extended to No. 2, previously the premises of the tea blenders, F. Broomhall and Co. After the move an optician's practice was added to the business on the first floor of No. 2. Fosters' remained in the Bull Ring until it was demolished to make way for the new post office. The business moved to Oxford Street for a while, opposite the Central Cinema, and then to the Swan Centre in Coventry Street after it was completed.

The business is currently owned by Mr Graham Hunt who followed his father into the business. Graham's grandmother married Evan Foster jnr after she was widowed when Graham's father was only an infant.

E. Foster & Son, after the move to 3 Bull Ring, c. 1916.

Evan Foster.   Mrs Foster.

Foster & Son, after they had acquired premises at 2 Bull Ring.

17, BULL RING, KIDDERMINSTER.

E. FOSTER,

PRACTICAL WATCH MAKER,

AND

Working Jeweller,

Begs to inform the Clergy, Gentry, and Inhabitants of Kidderminster and its neighbourhood that he has commenced business in the above line, and having had considerable experience in the English Lever Escapement Making, &c., Watches of the most delicate construction intrusted to him will be repaired and re-adjusted equal to new, at the lowest possible cost.

E. F. begs to invite an inspection of his
CAREFULLY-SELECTED STOCK OF

GOLD AND SILVER
ENGLISH LEVER WATCHES,
OF THE BEST MAKE.

GOLD JEWELLERY AND ELECTRO-PLATE
THE BEST QUALITY
KEPT IN STOCK.

CLOCKS WOUND IN THE COUNTRY AND KEPT IN REPAIR BY THE YEAR.

ESTIMATES GIVEN FOR RESILVERING OLD PLATE AND REGILDING JEWELLERY AS NEW.

Left: An early advertisement for Foster's shop. *Right*: Graham Hunt, the proprietor of Foster's shop, in the Swan Centre, 1998.

94

The Gas Showroom in the Bull Ring displayed cooking stoves, gas fires, water heaters, lighting fittings and refrigerators, all of which could be purchased with cash or on hire purchase terms. The lorries parked outside were fuelled by gas and they have gas bags on top. The Kidderminster Gas Company was one of the first of its type established in Great Britain: the inaugural meeting of the company was on 16 June 1818 and the original plant was in Pitts Lane. In 1903 4,100 consumers purchased gas. The company held a contract for lighting the streets and public buildings with twenty-one miles of mains that extended as far as Franche and Wolverley. Just prior to the Second World War, Cookley and Caunsall were also supplied.

The head office and works, Pitts Lane, c. 1934. The gas holder was erected in 1931 and was visible from much of the area.

The showroom interior. Right of centre is a gas range and on the left is the water boiler.

The gas holder, viewed from High Street, in the late 1940s.

The British Gas Energy Centre, High Street, 1999. After the Conservative Government sold gas and electricity back to the private sector in the 1990s it became possible to purchase gas from the electricity companies and vice versa.

THE HARVEY VACUUM CLEANERS CO., LTD.

Tel. 248.

Telegrams:
" Inventions."

The Original
and Oldest
Makers of
Vacuum
Cleaners in
the World.

Electric and
Hand Power
Vacuum
Cleaners for
Household
use, Hotels,
Theatres,
Libraries,
Shipping,
etc.

Agents in all Large
Towns.

Write for
Illustrations and
Name of nearest
Agent.

59/6

The Harvey Vacuum Cleaning Co. Ltd had their Kidderminster premises at 91 Coventry Street. Established in 1893, they continually improved their products and by the 1920s could be found all over the world. This advertisement dates from around 1921.

Mr and Mrs W.E. Timmis stand outside their shop in Coventry Street in 1895. They are surrounded by a splendid array of hardware and ironmonger's wares.

Littlebury's Business Directory for 1873 lists a John Tunstall of 10 Coventry Street as a lamp and oil dealer and *Kelly's Directory* for 1884 lists the same business at 89 Coventry Street. It appears that although the business was still in the same premises, the numbering had been changed. The business was actually established in 1865. In 1896 W.E. Timmis was listed as being at 90 Coventry Street. Ebenezer Timmis, the father of William Ebenezer Timmis, purchased the business from Mr Tunstall in 1889.

The business made steady progress and within a few years could provide household and furnishing goods, ironmonger's goods, fireplaces, stoves, tiled grates and general tools. By 1909 William Timmis' son, Beamer Timmis, had joined the firm and then, shortly after the First World War, the premises were extended to include ironmongery for builders. In 1935 the Timmis family made two very important decisions. They took on the Calor Gas agency and purchased an ironmonger's business in Load Street, Bewdley, from F.W. Mountford. One move complemented the other because the growing number of caravans in the area needed gas for heating and lighting. The caravans were mainly owned or rented by people from Birmingham who needed a break from the area where they worked and lived. They would come to Bewdley, Stourport, Arley and surrounding areas at weekends and holiday times and often still do today.

John Robert Timmis, the great grandson of the founder, joined the business in 1941 and, after hostilities had ceased in 1945, the Calor Gas business really took off. There would be a long queue in Load Street waiting to purchase essential fuel. At its peak they sold up to 1,600 32lb canisters per day, a far cry from collecting 6 per day from the railway station on Comberton Hill by horse and dray. Robert Timmis says that the intention was to maintain the Calor Gas around a third of total business the turnover, but at its peak it was nearer double this figure. Gas appliances and other sundries left at home by caravanners were bought from Timmis' firm.

There were, however, other reasons for the growing prosperity of the business. Trade was set up with the carpet factories after the Second World War, tools and hardware items were supplied to businesses including carpenters, plumbers and electricians, Birmingham Road and Rosemary Road were developed and council houses in the area were modernised.

In 1947 a number of caravanners were expected to arrive on a Sunday in need of Calor Gas. After having worked for six days, Robert Timmis did not relish the thought of opening on a Sunday. Instead, on Saturday Robert delivered a number of cylinders to the relevant sites and commissioned certain reputable caravanners as stockists, thus enabling him to have a well-deserved Sunday off.

The company had a reputation for looking after its staff. The Bewdley shop had only three managers in fifty-one years until it became R.G. Timmis, Bewdley Ltd. Three of the Kidderminster staff were prisoners of war in the Second World War, but that did not stop them from returning to Timmis' after 1945. One of the reasons for the company's closure in Kidderminster was that a number of the staff, including Robert Timmis himself were reaching retirement age with up to forty-eight years service.

R.G. Timmis is still trading in Bewdley, however, and hopefully will carry on well into the next millennium, keeping the name of Timmis alive in the area. The Bewdley shop has undergone great changes recently with the conversion of the rear of the premises into a mews of five specialised shop units. The mews has a walkway through to the municipal car park that makes it especially convenient for shoppers. A further development of the business is a trade ironmongery counter that offers specialist advice to the general builder. There is also a separate specialised shop unit in the mews known as 'Timmis Pots & Pans' which sells cookware and a recent addition known as 'Pencil Case' which sells stationery. Ironmongery and hardware is concentrated in the original shop on Load Street.

Timmis' shop, from Blackwell Street car park, in 1985.

Downton & Sons, 90-91 Coventry Street, was established in 1819. The firm were high-class furniture sellers, cabinetmakers, upholsterers, fitters of a wide variety of window blinds and expert paperhangers. There was a large warehouse for storing furniture and an important branch of their trade was the selling and laying of carpets. The works and repair shop were at Court 12, Coventry Street, and the total accommodation comprised an area of more than 5,000 square feet. The head of the firm in 1902 was Mr Alfred Good Downton who took over from his father in 1898. In a 1921 advertisement, Downtons offered potential customers the opportunity to visit their London warehouses where they would have an immense stock of goods to choose from. The offer included rail fare and carriage paid for all goods purchased.

J. & H. Russell,
Coventry Street.

After the First World War, radio fast became the new phenomena, just as television would in the 1950s. John and Harry Russell soon realised that a vast market of potential purchasers was opening up. They opened premises in Blackwell Street in 1929 (later the site of the telephone exchange) supplying receiver parts and offering a construction service for people who had neither the time nor the inclination to build their own set.

After some years the business moved to the Coventry Street location shown here, one of the oldest shop premises still existing in Kidderminster. The premises had previously been Wood's fish shop, next door to Allen's grocery shop. At one time music was played in and outside the shop but this stopped after complaints from neighbouring shopkeepers.

Around 1939 the business diversified and started selling cycles, holding agencies for Royal Enfield and Rudge Whitworth. When the circus came to town they were often called upon to repair the circus performers' cycles and Harry occasionally repaired the spikes on the local policeman's helmets. Sergeant Allen, PC Bert Jones and PC Broomfield were three known to take advantage of the service.

In the early days of the firm, new bicycles arrived at the railway station and were wheeled to the shop ready for assembly and sale. Events such as speed trials at Aggborough Stadium's cinder track and exhibitions at the Town Hall aroused the public's interest in cycling and helped to sell extra bicycles for Russell's.

Before electricity became normal in the average home, a large part of Russell's business involved charging accumulators used to power radios. These were delivered by bicycle with a carrier fitted to the front and rear. As business improved, a motorcycle and sidecar was purchased and later a car. In the early days large radiograms were collected and delivered by bicycle. The charging of accumulators ceased in the early 1950s when electricity became available in the majority of homes.

The electrical retail trade has probably witnessed more changes than most, especially since the post-war boom. Russell's has progressed a long way since John and Harry Russell first received the Marconi broadcasts in the area. The business is run today by the third generation, Stephen and Ian Russell. John Russell is semi-retired and deals mainly with the paperwork.

A collection of some of the radio sets built and sold by Russell's.

Left: John Russell (senior) repairing a bicycle at the rear of the Coventry Street shop. *Right*: John Russell junior and senior stand outside their Coventry Street shop.

The mosaic floor from the old entrance to Allen's grocery store, which Mr Russell has preserved. S.P.Q.R. stands for 'Small Profit Quick Return.'

Wright's cycle shop, situated on the left-hand side of Blackwell Street as you look towards the Horsefair, c. 1930.

The working staff of the Worcestershire Brewing & Malting Co. Ltd, Kidderminster, 1897. Built around 1850 on the site of a deep well, the firm was originally called Bucknall's Brewery. It was taken over by the Worcestershire Brewing and Malting Company, but brewing ceased under this name around 1913. Later the company became known as the Kidderminster Brewery before it was taken over by Banks'.

On the extreme right of the front row is George Humphries who lived in Lea Street and, in his younger days, was a keen boxer. On the extreme left of the middle row is Billy Button who ran away from his home in Flanders because his family wanted him to be a surgeon. His name was actually De Witt but this eventually changed to Dewick, probably from being misspelt. He adopted the name Button from the people he lodged with. Billy fought in the Sepoy Mutiny in India (1857-59) which led to the abolition of the East India Company in 1858 and the transfer of the administration of India to the British crown. He was injured in the leg, hence the crutch, but did receive the medals shown here for his fighting. Billy was a travelling salesman for the brewing company, selling wines and spirits, and later owned The Duke of Edinburgh in Bromsgrove Street which opened around 1879. He had four daughters and two sons. Next to him is Harry Robinson, one of his sons-in-law, and in the middle of the front row is one of Billy Button's sons, Albert Edward Dewick, the head brewer. Albert later kept a number of public houses in the town; the last one was the Rampant Lion in George Street which closed when he died in 1926. Another employee was Ernie Britton (probably fourth from the right on the middle row) who completed fifty years with the brewery by 1939. He worked in the cellars and also helped with the brewing. Ernie was allowed to continue working past the normal retirement age and finally left the company around 1950.

W. Meades, herbalist, 98 Blackwell Street. Herbal remedies are not a new fad but have been around for years. W. Meades was listed in *Kelly's Directory* at these premises from 1904 to 1928.

The Horsefair, looking towards Stourbridge Road, *c.* 1900.

Annie E. Taylor at the Navigation public house, Clensmore, around 1954, having completed fifty years of service with Banks' Brewery. The Navigation opened in 1881 and was probably built in anticipation of a railway line that was proposed from Stourbridge to Kidderminster via Pedmore, Belbroughton and Chaddesley Corbett. As the station was never built the Navigation was always considered to be something of a white elephant, built more for use as a hotel. There were lots of rooms that were never used. In spite of all this, it survived until 7 March 1973, drawing its trade from local factories and people who lived in the area. It was converted into offices and is still in use today. Annie Taylor passed away in 1956.

Mrs Taylor with some of her customers. At the front, second left is Doll Hall, second right is Jack Barber (Annie's son-in-law) and third right is Mrs Golding.

Four

The Flood of 1955

Stanley G. Stewart stands outside his off licence and confectionery shop in Mill Street, looking totally demoralised. The young boy in the right foreground is Geoff Jukes.

The highest flood recorded in Kidderminster occurred on 14 May 1886. The water was 5ft deep at Goodwins Mill and a little further up Mill Street it reached a depth of 5ft 10in. At the Town Hall it reached 18in up the base of Sir Rowland Hill's statue.

The flood of 27 March 1955 caused more damage due to the incredible rate at which the water rose and the lack of warning received from further up the River Stour. Normal flood precautions were taken on the Saturday evening. Town centre shop owners who could be contacted were warned and numerous sandbags were provided to seal doorways and help stem the flow of water. It was expected that the water would rise at the rate of 1 to 2 inches per hour but, as strenuous efforts were still being made to contact other property owners, the water level rose 18in between 3.45 and 4.30 on Sunday morning. It was 9in over the town bridge and when the canal burst its banks, it reached a depth of 2ft over the Trinity Lane Bridge.

Mr John L. Evans, the Town Clerk at the time, was rowed across to the Town Hall. On his arrival he proceeded to remove his trousers and waded down into the strong room where he managed to rescue two boxes and several bundles of documents. These included a George IV document which had survived, despite being completely submerged in the water.

At the library on Market Street the newly made archives, where Kidderminster's old records were kept, were flooded to a depth of almost 3ft. Many unique and irreplaceable documents were destroyed. It was ironic that in their centenary year they should suffer so great a loss. The Borough Librarian at that time was Mr. L.W. Horsfall.

The fire brigade helped to take food to people marooned in their houses in Mill Street by placing ladders up to their upstairs windows. Some people had five to six feet of water in their homes. The town's policemen took on the job of ferry men and, as the day wore on, became so adept at rowing that they started to seriously consider entering the next Bewdley Regatta.

The carpet factories most affected were Carpet Trades, Brintons, and C.M. Co. Ltd but these were all back in production within eight days. At Brintons the water was 3in deep in the weaving sheds while at Slingfield they managed to stop the rise of the water by knocking holes in the walls and allowing the water to run out into the canal.

The Bull Ring with Foster's the jewellers on the left and Blunt's shoe shop to the left of Keys'. Mr P. Hunt, the manager of Foster's, had the foresight to remove stock from the lower shelves and windows. This limited the damage, even though the water flooded his shop to a depth of 2ft.

A view along Trinity Lane. The windows on the left are where T.J. Hughes is now situated. The bridge over the Stour was completely submerged. The water reached a depth of 3ft at F.A. Kettle the stationers (not visible in this photograph). The swirling water tossed cabinets and counters around causing damage in excess of £500.

Vicar Street, looking towards the Town Hall.

The Fifty Shilling Tailors, Vicar Street. The men in the boat are Ted Gamson and policeman, Dick Hill. The policeman in the helmet is George Powell (number K16), a member of the old Kidderminster police force. The Fifty Shilling Tailors were one of the worst hit businesses in this part of town, incurring extensive damage to suits, yards of cloth and, ironically, hundreds of raincoats. Another loss was the damage to the display dummies that had stood in the water for so long that their bases deteriorated, causing them to suddenly collapse.

The Futurist cinema on Vicar Street was completely flooded downstairs to a depth of 8ft in the stage area and reached 18in up the curtains. All the seats had to be removed and 500 were replaced. The cinema was closed for well over a week with losses in excess of £1,500, including takings.

On the left-hand side of Park Butts is Thompson & Parkes, the builders, merchants and ironmongers. According to the manager, Mr Gorfankl, the loss in equipment and stock was huge, perhaps in excess of £2,000. Some of the stock was carried away by the torrent and the basement, which housed the bathroom furniture, was still flooded on the following Wednesday. Would it have been better to have left the plugs in the bathroom suites or not?

John Leavesley, nicknamed Lofty because he stands at 6ft 6in, certainly chose an occupation suited to his height. Lofty has been cleaning shop windows in Kidderminster for over thirty years. After leaving the Royal Navy in the middle of the 1960s he delivered bread on a wage of £12 5s 11d per week. After delivering for three months he decided to start up a window-cleaning round. It was not difficult to get customers as people who were in full employment did not have time to clean windows. Lofty started off earning £13 per week, but after about six months things really started to improve and he has been fully employed ever since. Today there is more work from the various stores in Kidderminster but more competition to get it.

Five
Sport and Leisure

The baths in Mill Street opened in 1855 and could be found next to the Town Mills. They consisted of a swimming bath that measured 37ft by 23ft 6in. In 1871 a Turkish bath was also added.

The open-air swimming pool, better known as the 'Resser', was situated where Reservoir Road is today. In the early 1950s it was a breeding ground for frogs!

The public swimming baths in New Road were erected in 1932 to replace the Mill Street baths. In later years the swimming area was boarded over at certain times of the year. Dancing, wrestling and five-a-side football were held and these events were always well supported.

This photograph of Kidderminster Harriers was taken before a match in the 1968/69 season when the team was one of the clubs greatest. Back row, left to right: R. Scott, F. Buxton, C. Smith, A. Wilcox, T. Jewkes, V. Cockcroft, R. Watson, S. Lloyd (coach). Front row: D. Gilbert, B. Wassall, P. Wassall, L. Cocker, B. Taylor, C. Pearson (trainer). John Henderson was missing due to injury; his place was taken by R. Scott.

Kidderminster Harriers greatest season was probably 1993/94. This is action from the fifth round FA Cup tie when the Harriers were narrowly beaten 1-0 by the mighty West Ham in front of nearly 8,000 people. They had disposed of Preston North End and Barry Fry's Birmingham City in earlier rounds.

Delwyn Humphreys caps a superb season when he lifts the Conference Championship Trophy in May 1994. This should have gained the Harriers entry to the Football League but, because the ground was not up to standard, it was not to be. Cruel luck indeed.

The Carpet Trades hockey team, *c.* 1951. Back row, left to right: Pecker Clarke, -?-, Stuart Parkes, Charlie Baker, -?-, Jack Barber. Front row: -?-, Tommy Teague, Frank Bishop, -?-, -?-.

The Carpet Trades football team, *c.* 1953. Back row, left to right: Perce Hudson, Joey Farmer, -?-, Roger Underwood, Dave Morris, Geoff Bourne. Front row: W. Chatterton, Alan Evans, Gilly Brooks, -?-, Len Millichip, Bobby Hunter, Sam Harvey.

Brinton Park Bowling Club, *c.* 1949. Back row, third left is Bill Williams, fourth right is P. Hudson and fifth right is F. Hudson. Front row, second left is Mr Lampitt and sitting on the extreme right is Mr French.

The original S.D.F. football team, 1957/58. Back Row, left to right: Sam Hughes, Peter Overfield, Bob Sparks, Vic Bowen, Geoff Sparks, Roy Houghton. Front row: Michael Bennett, Scotty Young, Ray Poole, Roger Haycock, Barry Houghton, Mick Thomson.

The Victoria cricket team were the beaten finalists of the Carpet Weavers Cup, *c.* 1958. Back row, left to right: J. Wadeley, S. Williams, -?-, G. Needham, B. Walker, G. Kershaw, R. Hatton. Front row: K. Stooke, C. Tovey, J. Freeman, R. Haycock. The two umpires are unknown.

Hoobrook Olympic, the winners of the Birmingham Junior Cup, the Worcester Junior Cup, and holders of the Kidderminster Weavers Cup and the Infirmary Cup. Back row, -?-, -?-, -?-, J. Houghton. Second row: -?-, S. Mayall, C. Pearsall, ? Arnold, Jim Tipper, T. Lloyd, D. Seers, H. Gould, J. Jefford. Third row: W. Tipper, C. Cookson, G. Morris, W. Gould, W. Grove, -?-, Jack Tipper. Front row: F. Barber, H. Lockley, B. Cope, T. Hayes, B. Cowell, F. Chell.

Brian Wilson's Sounds Around record and tape centre, Swan Centre, 1972.

Brian Wilson was born in 1938. He started work as a radio-engineering apprentice for F.W. Long in Mill Street in 1955 after attending King Charles grammar school. He served in the shop on occasions and eventually took the business over in 1967 when Mr Long retired. In 1972 the business was moved to the Swan Centre and a very up-to-date music store was set up. By 1987 they stocked over 10,000 LP and cassette titles of all types of music. Indeed, it probably had one of the most comprehensive ranges in the West Midlands around this time.

Brian and his wife Anna normally had three assistants with an extra two drafted in on Saturdays. The business also provided a special service for DJs that included discounts, free advertising and promotional singles. It also held a ticket agency for most NEC and Birmingham Odeon concerts.

In 1960, when local pop groups started to appear, he set up Startime Promotions with Martin Stook. This lasted until 1966, working mainly with Cliff Ward and The Cruisers, and Tommy and The Crestas at four main venues: the Mare and Colt, Town Hall, Chateau Impney and Bleak House (which later became Severn Manor). Sounds Around closed in 1993 due to the high rent that was asked for the shop.

On the right, Brian Wilson serves a customer in Sounds Around, *c.* 1987. Just a small selection of the audio and literary material is visible.

THE LOCAL TOP TEN

1. **I FEEL FINE** (3)
   Beatles
2. **I'M GONNA BE STRONG** (2)
   Gene Pitney
3. **LITTLE RED ROOSTER** (1)
   Rolling Stones
4. **I UNDERSTAND** (—)
   Freddie and the Dreamers
5. **WALK TALL** (10)
   Val Doonican
6. **ALL DAY AND ALL OF THE NIGHT** (6)
   Kinks
7. **DOWN TOWN** (4)
   Petula Clark
8. **BABY LOVE** (7)
   Supremes
9. **THERE'S A HEARTACHE FOLLOWING ME** (8)
   Jim Reeves
10. **PRETTY PAPER** (—)
    Roy Orbison

This list is compiled from sales information supplied by F. W. Long, Mill Street, Ronald Wilson & Co., Blackwell Street, Perry's Electrical (Stourport), Bewdley Electrical Industries and Boots (Kidderminster).

The local Top Ten from a 1964 edition of the *Kidderminster Shuttle* featured a number of famous bands that are still prominent today.

Cliff Ward and The Cruisers at the Black Horse Hotel, Mill Street. Left to right: Trevor Jones, Graham Drew, Rodney Simmonds, Butch Bowen, Cliff Ward. The group formed around 1960. There was always a great debate about whether 'the Crestas' or 'the Cruisers' were the most popular in the area. The name was later changed to Martyn Raynor and The Secrets when they recorded *Candy to Me*. The group eventually split to form the nucleus of The Reflections who, in time, probably gained more popularity. Cliff went on to achieve success as Clifford T. Ward. He had a number eight hit with *Gaye* which had eleven weeks on the charts in 1973. As a prolific songwriter, he also made a number of albums and some of his material was recorded by Jack Jones, notably *Home Thoughts From Abroad*. Though he achieved more than most local pop groups could dream about, he never quite had the success his talent deserved.

A variety of Christmas and New Year attractions could be seen at the Park Attwood Hotel in 1964 including Cliff Ward and The Cruisers.

PARK ATTWOOD HOTEL

★ ## Christmas Attractions ★

CHRISTMAS EVE

DANCE TO THE BARONS

7/6 : Bar Extension till 1.0 a.m.

BOXING NIGHT

BUFFET DANCE with SPOT PRIZES : 15/-
CLIFF WARD and THE CRUISERS
Buffet 10.30 : Bar Extension till 12 midnight

NEW YEAR'S EVE

CARNIVAL NIGHT 21/-

BUFFET and WINE : THE SCORPIONS
Buffet & Wine 10.30. Bar extension till 2.0 a.m.

DRESS OPTIONAL : TICKETS ONLY
Tickets Available now from
PARK ATTWOOD HOTEL, TRIMPLEY

Tommy and The Crestas, c. 1963. Front row, left to right: Dave Mansfield, Nigel Bache, Tim Wilson. Back row: Nigel Turrall, Tommy Noise. The Fender guitars of the type seen here are worth a small fortune today. Formed around 1960, the group still exists today. Two of the original members, Nigel Bache and Nigel Turrall, are still in the line up and Dave Mansfield has only recently decided to call it a day. He is, however, already missing the performing. The band's popularity was due to their clean, crisp sound, an ability to keep up with the latest charts and an ability to entertain. When Tommy left the group they were joined by Pete Hazelwood. In the early sixties Pete appeared on television under the name of Peter Wynne in Jack Goode's *Oh Boy* alongside such stars as Cliff Richard, Marty Wilde and the late great, Billy Fury.

123

The Gamblers, *c.* 1960. Left to right: Graham Phillpotts, Terry Davies, Roger Bayliss, John Wainwright, Ken Chatterton. Occasionally, Roger Jackson would be in the line-up on piano. He achieved fame in The Tornados who had a number one smash hit with *Telstar* in August 1962, produced by the legendary Joe Meek. The idea for a letter G embroidered on each jacket came from watching a performance of The Clippers. The G varies on each because a design was not agreed beforehand. You can just imagine the look on their faces at the next gig!

The Reflections, *c.* 1968. Left to right: Bruce Ward, Pete Rowley, Trevor Jones, Paul Mackreath, Graham Drew, Roger Shapcott. The Reflections formed in 1966 and were a spin-off from Cliff Ward and The Cruisers. Over the years they had many different line-ups. They were always a very busy band and had loyal followers.

Jess and The Raiders. Left to right: Jess Roden, Mick Thomas, Chris Hayes, Colin Hepwood, Rob Newell. The Raiders formed around 1962, mainly through the efforts of Colin Hepwood. They started off playing music by artists such as Eddie Cochran and The Shadows. While the majority of would-be musicians had to be content with practising in someone's front room, The Raiders were very fortunate in having Frank Freeman's ballroom at their disposal. The group broke up when Jess Roden joined Shakedown Sound and later went on to turn professional with the Alan Bown Set. Though Jess never really hit the heights in the UK he enjoyed some success in New York where he spent a number of years.

The Indigo Set looking very trendy in a publicity shot for Mister Casual at the lower end of Worcester Street in July 1966. Left to right: Alan Attwood (rhythm guitar), Ian Hardiman (lead guitar), Martin Harrison (drums), Rob Newell (bass), Colin Youngjohns (vocalist).

The Crown and Anchor, situated on the corner of Broad Street and Jerusalem Walk, was a Bucknall's public house. The licensee was Albert E. Dewick, the former head brewer at Bucknall's Brewery. It opened around 1855 and closed in 1933.

The Britannia in Blackwell Street opened around 1855 and closed in 1909. This was another of Bucknall's public houses: the brewery was just over the road. The licensee at the time of this photograph was a Mr Westwood.

The Yew Tree on Barnsleys Hill, Broadwaters, opened around 1903. The Yew Tree, the Britannia and the Crown and Anchor were places where it was possible to relax and spend some time at leisure.

Brinton Crescent and Woodward Road viewed from the Serpentine. In the right background is the Spinney. There were two ponds that survived from Sutton Farm until they were drained and filled in during the 1950s. Many hours were passed away here by the local children playing cricket, football and rounders, ice skating during a cold winter or just chasing each other about in typical childlike fashion.

This last view of the demolition of the Bull Ring in 1965, taken from the gas holder, shows the continually changing nature of Kidderminster.

Acknowledgements

The author wishes to extend his gratitude to the following for the use of photographs and providing information: Miss L.K. Hart, Mrs S. Brown and the helpful staff of the Kidderminster Reference Library, the *Kidderminster Shuttle*, H.J. Higgott, Mrs J. Bradley and the late Gerry Bradley, Tony and Pat Chambers, Peter and Russell at Pritchard's, 22 Oxford Street, Mr R. Thompson, Terry and Bern, the late Annie Hall, Geoff and Christine Jukes, Ron Lewis, Graham Turner, Graham Hunt at Foster's Jewellers, Mrs Tomkinson, Bob Timmis, Miss J. Hodge, Tony Ray, Mr Hunter, Graham Hughes and Wolverhampton Wanderers Football Club, the staff at the British Gas Energy Centre, the late Graham Searl, Mr Ronald Edwards, Geoff Edwards, Janet Robinson, John Russell, Barry Onslow, Perce Hudson, Cliff Brown, Dee Knight, D.T.N. Booth, Trevor Jones, Ian Hardiman, Roger Bayliss, Dave Mansfield, Jerry Cashmore, Colin Youngjohns, Kidderminster Harriers FC, Roger Haycock, Brian Wilson at Sounds Around, Rob Newell, Mrs Canning and Mrs Strupinski, the late Nigel Crowther, G. Wormald.